Pebble

Countries

Mexico

by Christine Juarez

Consulting Editor: Gail Saunders-Smith, PhD

CAPSTONE PRESS
a capstone imprint

Pebble Books are published by Capstone Press,
1710 Roe Crest Drive, North Mankato, Minnesota 56003
www.capstonepub.com

Library of Congress Cataloging-in-Publication Data
Juarez, Christine, 1976–
  Mexico / by Christine Juarez.
     pages cm.—(Pebble books. Countries)
  Includes bibliographical references and index.
  Summary: "Simple text and full-color photographs illustrate the land, animals, and people of
Mexico"—Provided by publisher.
  ISBN 978-1-4765-3516-6 (paperback)
  1. Mexico—Juvenile literature. I. Title.
  F1208.5.J83 2014
  972—dc23   2013002014

Editorial Credits
Erika L. Shores, editor; Bobbie Nuytten, designer; Wanda Winch, media researcher;
Jennifer Walker, production specialist

Photo Credits
Capstone, 4, 22 (currency); Corbis: Royalty-Free, 19; Dreamstime: Jerl71, 15, Richard Gunion,
17; Shutterstock: Eduardo Rivero, 9, f9photos, 21, Frontpage, 5, Joao Virissimo, cover, Matty
Symons, 1,7, Melaics, cover, 1 (design element), movit, 22 (flag), Ohmega1982, back cover globe,
Sumikophoto, 13, tipograffias, 11

Note to Parents and Teachers

The Countries set supports national social studies standards related to
people, places, and culture. This book describes and illustrates Mexico.
The images support early readers in understanding the text. The repetition
of words and phrases helps early readers learn new words. This book
also introduces early readers to subject-specific vocabulary words, which
are defined in the Glossary section. Early readers may need assistance to
read some words and to use the Table of Contents, Glossary, Read More,
Internet Sites, and Index sections of the book.

Printed in the United States of America in North Mankato, Minnesota.
032013   007223CGF13

Table of Contents

Where Is Mexico?

Mexico is a country in North America. Mexico is south of the United States. The capital of Mexico is Mexico City.

MEXICO

Mexico City

Landforms and Climate

Sandy beaches line Mexico's coasts. Mexico also has deserts, rain forests, and mountains. The weather in Mexico is mostly warm and dry.

Animals

Many kinds of animals live in
Mexico. Golden eagles nest
in trees. Toucans live in Mexico's
rain forests. Coyotes live in
the deserts and mountains.

Language and Population

More than 116 million people live in Mexico. Most Mexicans live in cities. Spanish is the country's official language.

Food

Many Mexicans buy their food at outdoor markets. They buy chili peppers, bananas, and beans. People enjoy tortillas, tacos, and rice.

Celebrations

Mexicans celebrate the Day of the Dead. This holiday is in November. Families visit the graves of their loved ones. They bring flowers and food.

Where People Work

Most Mexicans work in service businesses such as tourism. Other Mexicans work in stores and factories. Farmers grow wheat, coffee, cotton, corn, and fruit.

Transportation

Most Mexicans travel in cars
and buses. Taxis are busy
in cities too. In the mountains,
people ride horses.

CIRCUITO INTE

← CHAPUL

Famous Sight

Thousands of years ago, people in Mexico built huge stone pyramids. Some pyramids are still standing. Visitors climb many steps to reach each pyramid's top.

Country Facts

Name: United Mexican States

Capital: Mexico City

Population: 116,220,947 (July 2013 estimate)

Size: 758,449.43 square miles
(1,964,375 square kilometers)

Language: Spanish

Main Crops: corn, wheat, rice, beans, coffee, fruit

Money: Mexican peso

Mexico's flag

Glossary

capital—the city in a country where the government is based

chili pepper—a small, spicy food used to flavor spicy sauces

coast—land next to an ocean or sea

desert—a very dry area of land

factory—the place where a product, such as a car, is made

grave—the place where a dead person is buried

language—the way people speak or talk

North America—the continent that includes the United States, Canada, Mexico, and Central America

official—having the approval of a country or a certain group of people

pyramid—a structure that is big at the bottom and small at the top; many of the pyramids in Mexico have steps

rain forest—a tropical forest where a lot of rain falls

tortilla—a round, flat bread

tourism—the business of taking care of visitors to a country or place

Read More

Sexton, Colleen. *Mexico*. Exploring Countries. Minneapolis: Bellwether Media, 2011.

Stalcup, Ann. *Mexico in Colors*. World of Colors. Mankato, Minn.: Capstone Press, 2009.

Streissguth, Thomas. *Mexico*. Country Explorers. Minneapolis: Lerner, 2008.

Internet Sites

FactHound offers a safe, fun way to find Internet sites related to this book. All of the sites on FactHound have been researched by our staff.

Here's all you do:
Visit *www.facthound.com*
Type in this code: 9781476530765

Check out projects, games and lots more at
www.capstonekids.com

Index

Word Count: 201   Grade: 1   Early-Intervention Level: 18